Ancient Greeks

Stephanie Turnbull

Designed by Catherine-Anne MacKinnon
and Vici Leyhane

Illustrated by Colin King

Additional design by Helen Wood and Laura Parker

Additional illustrations by Uwe Mayer

Greek consultant: Dr. Katharine Haynes

Reading consultant: Alison Kelly

Contents

An ancient land

Greece is a hot country in southern Europe. The ancient Greeks lived there about three thousand years ago.

Many Greek towns were near the sea. Boats carried people from place to place.

Life in Greece

Some Greeks lived in busy towns or cities. Others lived far out in the countryside.

This is how a small Greek town might have looked.

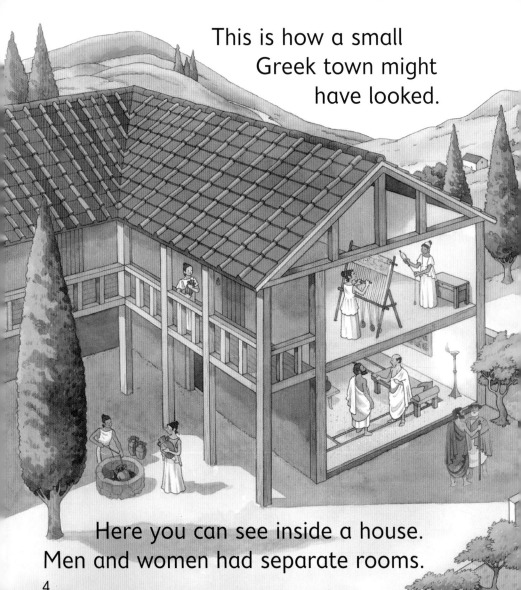

Here you can see inside a house. Men and women had separate rooms.

Temples and other important buildings stood on hills.

Greek houses were made of wood and mud bricks.

Rich people had slaves to do the housework for them.

5

Clothes and fashion

The Greeks liked to wear simple, loose clothes that kept them cool.

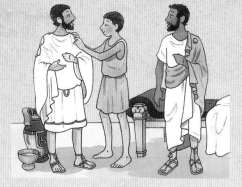

Women always wore long tunics called chitons.

Men wore long or short tunics, often with a cloak.

Rich women had earrings like these, made from gold.

This ancient Greek statue shows a woman dressed in outdoor clothes.

She is wearing a sunhat and a cloak to protect her from the Sun.

Many Greek men had beards. It was fashionable to keep them neatly trimmed.

What people ate

Most Greek people ate lots of vegetables, fruit and other fresh foods.

This Greek clay model shows a woman stirring food in a big pot.

She is probably making a fish or vegetable stew.

Farmers grew crops that were used for making bread.

Often people kept a few goats and sheep for their milk.

People who lived near the sea caught fresh fish to eat.

There were plenty of olives to knock down from olive trees.

Poor people just ate lumpy porridge made from flour and water.

A trip to market

The market was the busiest part of every ancient Greek town.

At the market there were lots of stalls selling fresh food.

People stood and chatted with friends or had meetings.

The Greeks paid for their shopping with silver coins like these.

Slaves stood on a round platform, waiting to be sold.

Craftsmen sold all kinds of pots from their workshops.

Feasts and fun

The Greeks loved to have big feasts.
Usually these parties were just for men.

As visitors arrived, slaves washed their
hands and feet.

Everyone ate plenty of meat, fish, cheese
and vegetables, then fruit and cakes.

The guests stayed for hours, drinking
wine and talking.

Men played a game where they threw wine at a target.

If they missed, they had to have another drink and try again.

Some feasts had music too. This painting of a Greek party shows a musician playing two flutes.

Gods and goddesses

The Greeks believed in many gods and goddesses, and told hundreds of stories about them.

This is a statue of Artemis, the Greek goddess of hunting.

She lived in the forest and hunted animals with arrows.

Zeus was the king of the gods. He was married to Hera, a beautiful goddess.

Zeus' brother, Poseidon, ruled the sea. He lived in an underwater palace.

Athene was Zeus' daughter. She was the strict, wise goddess of war.

Hades was king of the Underworld, where all dead people were taken.

If Zeus was angry with someone, he hurled lightning down at them.

15

Talking to the gods

Gods and goddesses were very important to the Greeks.

In temples, people prayed to statues of gods for help.

They also brought presents to make the gods happy.

There were festivals for gods, with music, dancing and sports.

Priestesses gave people messages from the gods.

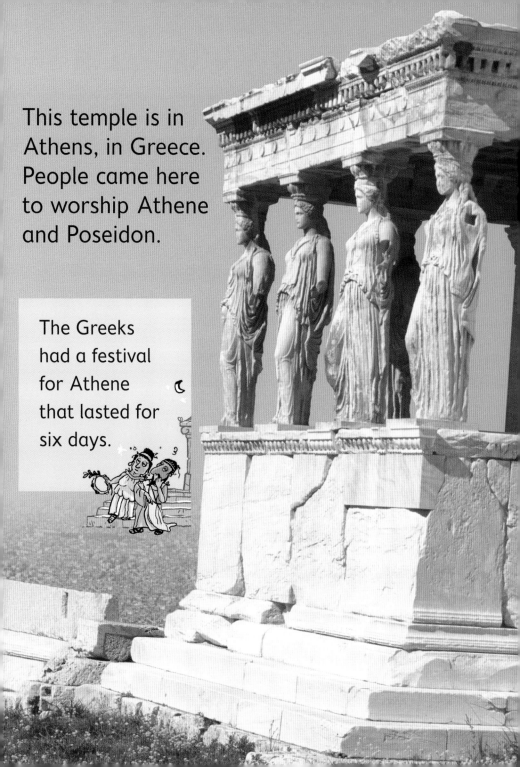

This temple is in Athens, in Greece. People came here to worship Athene and Poseidon.

The Greeks had a festival for Athene that lasted for six days.

Heroes and monsters

There are many myths about brave Greek heroes and the terrible beasts they fought.

The monster Medusa turned men to stone if they looked at her.

A clever young man named Perseus set out to kill Medusa.

He used his shield as a mirror, so he never looked at her.

Perseus cut off the monster's head and came home a hero.

This painting from a pot shows a hero called Heracles, killing a terrifying monster.

Heracles was half-man and half-god, which made him very strong.

The Olympic Games

The Olympic Games began in Olympia, in ancient Greece. They were made up of many sports. They still exist today.

These runners are taking part in the modern Olympics.

At the ancient Olympics there were wrestling matches.

Some athletes hurled a discus as far as they could.

The modern Olympics are held all over the world. Only the best athletes take part.

Another popular Olympic sport was the long jump.

Men raced around a track in chariots pulled by horses.

Greek plays

Many Greeks enjoyed going to see plays,
which were shown outside.

People sat in rows
on stone seats.

The actors had lots
of space to perform.

People watched plays here in ancient times.
You can still see seats and part of the stage.

Greek actors wore masks to show what their characters were like. This mask shows a funny old man.

Some plays were tragedies. These had a sad ending.

Other plays were comedies, which made people laugh.

Only men were allowed to act in plays.

Mighty warriors

Some Greek men trained to be soldiers.
A few soldiers rode on horses, but many
others marched on foot.

This picture from a Greek pot shows foot
soldiers fighting with long, pointed spears.

24

A Greek soldier wore metal plates to protect his body.

Metal plates called greaves were strapped to his legs.

A large helmet covered his head and neck.

He carried a sharp spear and a flat metal shield.

Soldiers had swords too. This is a modern copy of a Greek sword and its holder.

Into battle

The Greeks had wars with other countries, and sometimes with each other too.

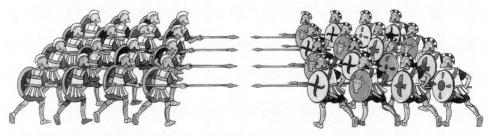

Most of the fighting was done on foot. Groups of soldiers charged at each other.

Soldiers often attacked enemy cities. They broke down the walls and stormed in.

There were many sea battles. Ships called triremes tried to ram each other.

This modern ship has been built to look just like an ancient Greek trireme.

People sit inside the ship and row with long oars.

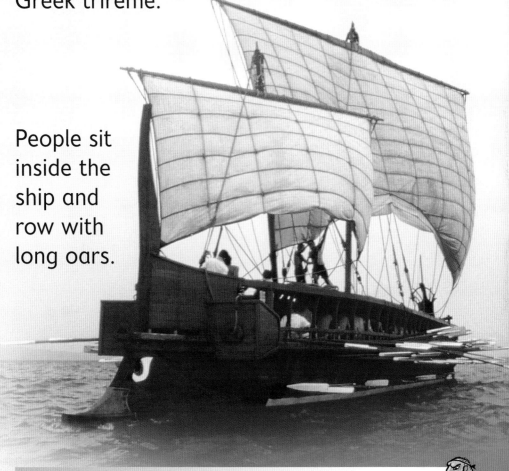

One part of Greece, called Sparta, was famous for its strong, fearless fighters.

Great Greeks

Many clever people lived in ancient Greece.

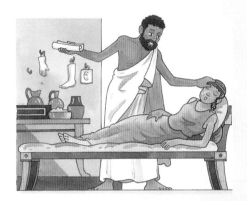

Hippocrates was a doctor who learned how bodies worked.

Aristotle studied science and wrote many books.

Sappho was a rich woman who wrote beautiful poems.

Pericles was a wise leader who ruled the city of Athens.

Alexander the
Great was a brave soldier.
This picture shows him riding into battle.

Alexander always
wanted to be a hero.

When he grew up, he
ruled all of Greece.

Some Greeks were inventors, but
many of their machines didn't work.

Glossary

Here are some of the words in this book you might not know. This page tells you what they mean.

 temple - a place where the ancient Greeks prayed to statues of gods.

 chiton - a long or short dress made from one piece of material.

 priestess - a woman who worked in a temple and spoke to the gods.

 shield - a flat metal plate. Soldiers used shields to protect themselves.

 discus - a round metal or stone plate used in throwing competitions.

 chariot - a small cart with two wheels that was pulled by horses.

 trireme - a powerful Greek warship with three rows of oars on each side.

Usborne Quicklinks

Would you like to find out more about the ancient Greeks? You can visit Usborne Quicklinks for links to websites with videos, amazing facts and things to make and do.

Go to **usborne.com/Quicklinks** and type in the keywords **"beginners ancient Greeks"**.
Make sure you ask a grown-up before going online.

Notes for grown-ups

Please read the internet safety guidelines at Usborne Quicklinks with your child. Children should be supervised online. The websites are regularly reviewed and the links at Usborne Quicklinks are updated. However, Usborne Publishing is not responsible and does not accept liability for the content or availability of any website other than its own.

This Greek jug is 2,600 years old. It has an animal's head for its spout.

Index

Acknowledgements

Photographic manipulation by Mike Wheatley

Photo credits

The publishers are grateful to the following for permission to reproduce material.
Cover © Procession of horsemen, 445-438 BC, by Phidias, Detail/British Museum, London, UK/
De Agostini Picture Library/Bridgeman Images; **p1** © The Art Archive/Kanellopoulos Museum Athens/Dagli Orti; **p6** ©
The Trustees of the British Museum; **p7** © The Trustees of the British Museum; **p8** © CM Dixon/Heritage Images; **p11** ©
The Art Archive/Kanellopoulos Museum Athens/Dagli Orti; **p13** © The Art Archive/Bibliothèque des Arts Décoratifs Paris/
Dagli Orti; **p14** © The Bridgeman Art Library/The Louvre/Peter Willi; **p17** © Alamy/Webphotographer/Nebojsa Basic; **p19**
© The Trustees of the British Museum; **p20-21** © Corbis/Le Segretain Pascal/Corbis Sygma; **p22** © Corbis/Roger Wood;
p23 © The Art Archive/ Archaeological Museum Piraeus/Dagli Orti; **p24** © The Art Archive/National Archaeological
Museum Athens/Dagli Orti; **p25** © Ancient-Empires.com; **p27** © Ancient Art and Architecture Collection/Mike Andrews;
p29 © Corbis/Mimmo Jodice; **p31** © The Trustees of the British Museum

Sun, moon and stars

Farm animals

Elizabeth I

Rubbish & Recycling

Dogs

Horses and ponies

Spiders

Planes

Cats

Ancient Greeks

VOLCANOES

DINOSAURS

Your Body

Armour

Sharks

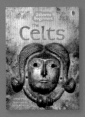
The Celts

VIKINGS

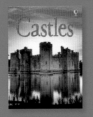
Castles

How flowers grow

Digging up the past

Caterpillars & Butterflies

Ballet

Pirates

EGYPTIANS

Eggs & Chicks

ROMANS

Weather

Tadpoles & Frogs

Why do we eat?

Under the sea

Bears

AZTECS

TRUCKS

Night Animals

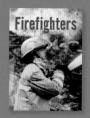
Firefighters

Antarctica

Bugs

COWBOYS

PLANET EARTH

London

Seashore

China

Dangerous Animals

Rainforests

Trees

Reptiles

Ships

Bats

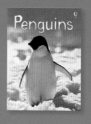
Penguins

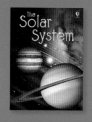
The Solar System

Knights

Monkeys

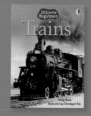
Trains

Elephants

Tigers

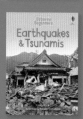
Earthquakes & Tsunamis

Storms and Hurricanes

BEES & WASPS

Wolves

Owls